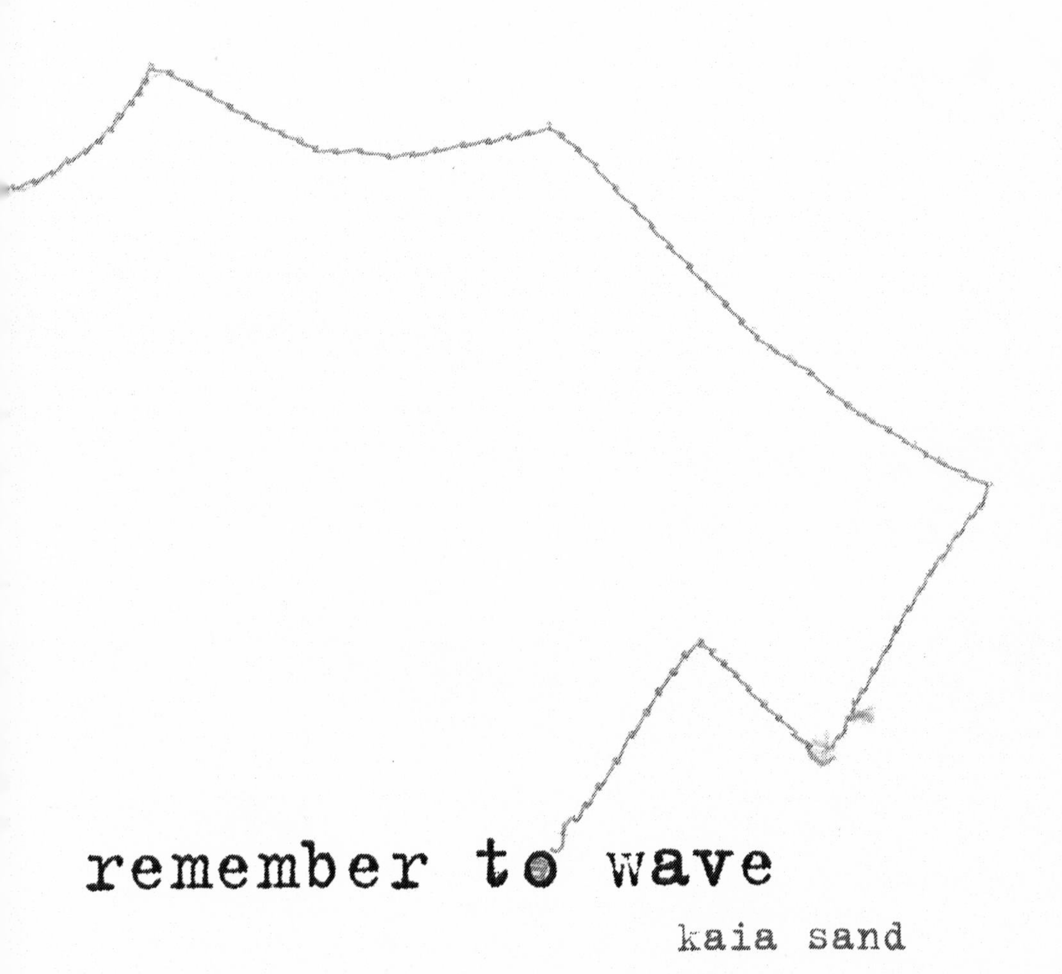

remember to wave

kaia sand

TINFISH

TinFish Press
Susan M. Schultz, Editor
47-728 Hui Kelu Street #9
Kāneʻohe, HI 96744

www.tinfishpress.com

Cover art and book design by Bao Hoa Nguyen
Map collage and stitching by Kaia Sand

ISBN 978-0-9789929-8-9
0-9789929-8-9

I dedicate this book to Neal Sand, who walks the brush and knows the squats (my flâneur with a conscience); Meg Eberle Ainsworth, whose motivated curiosity inspires my poet-journalist bent; Jules Boykoff, who walks & thinks & writes with me in our daily ease & joyful intensity; and Jessica Wahnetah, who wonders open my world with humor & dreaming & wisdom. I dedicate this walk-poem to you & you & you & you.

To those who were held prisoner in the Portland Assembly Center, and to those whose lives were ended or rent by the Vanport flood—to you I acknowledge a responsibility. Here is one small attempt at addressing that responsibility through committed inquiry, through pedestrian investigation.

Thank you to everyone at Tinfish Press, especially Susan Schultz, who patiently stewarded this project from our early conversations, and Bao Hoa Nguyen, whose design intelligence and creativity helped me realize this book.

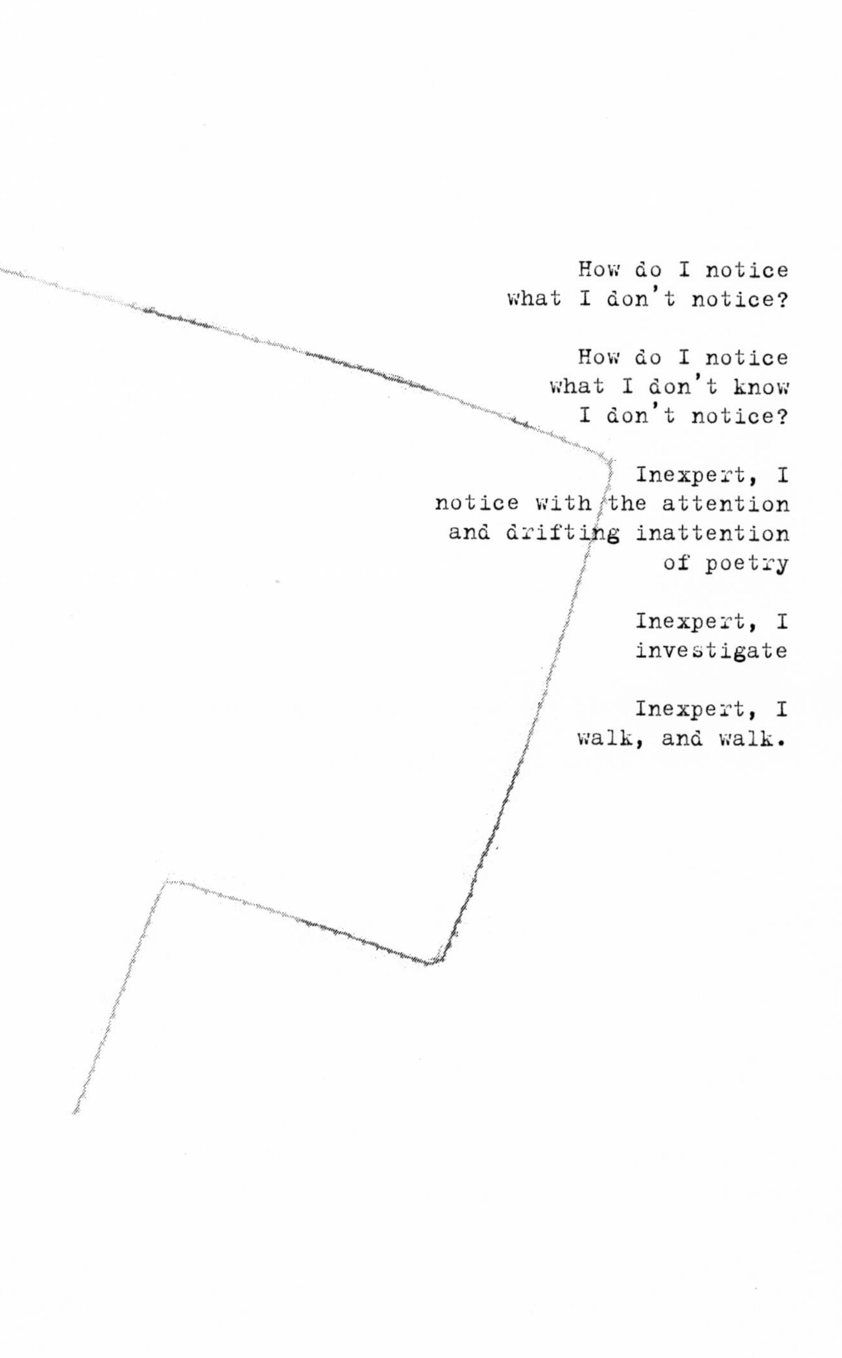

How do I notice
what I don't notice?

How do I notice
what I don't know
I don't notice?

Inexpert, I
notice with the attention
and drifting inattention
of poetry

Inexpert, I
investigate

Inexpert, I
walk, and walk.

1.REMEMBER TO WAVE
a poetry walk

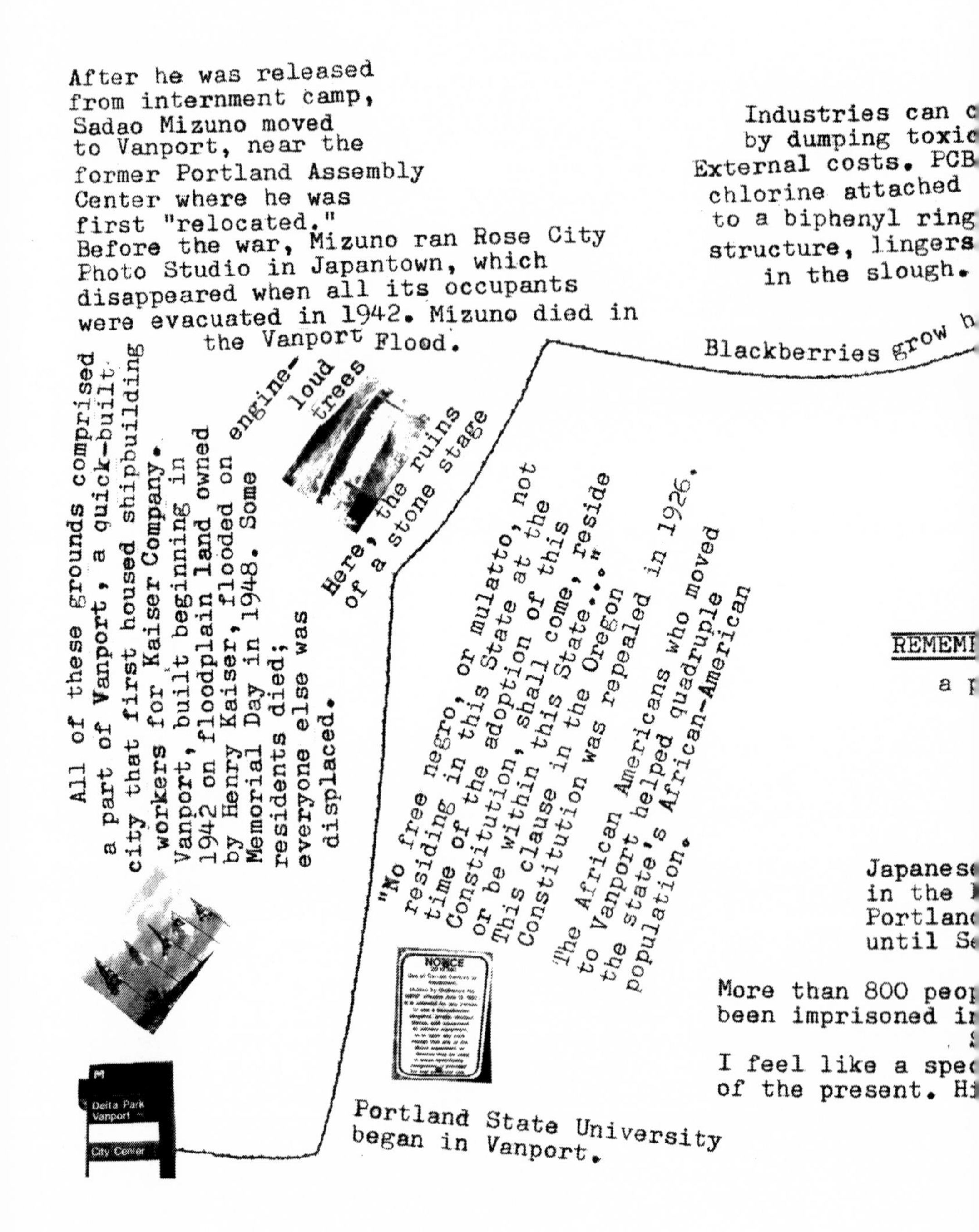

After he was released
from internment camp,
Sadao Mizuno moved
to Vanport, near the
former Portland Assembly
Center where he was
first "relocated."
Before the war, Mizuno ran Rose City
Photo Studio in Japantown, which
disappeared when all its occupants
were evacuated in 1942. Mizuno died in
the Vanport Flood.
Industries can c
by dumping toxic
External costs. PCB
chlorine attached
to a biphenyl ring
structure, lingers
in the slough.
Blackberries grow h
All of these grounds comprised
a part of Vanport, a quick-built
city that first housed shipbuilding
workers for Kaiser Company.
Vanport, built beginning in
1942 on floodplain land owned
by Henry Kaiser, flooded on
Memorial Day in 1948. Some
residents died;
everyone else was
displaced.
engine-
loud
trees
Here, the ruins
of a stone stage
"No free negro, or mulatto, not
residing in this State at the
time of the adoption of this
Constitution, shall come, reside
or be within this State...."
This clause in the Oregon
Constitution was repealed in 1926.
The African Americans who moved
to Vanport helped quadruple
the state's African-American
population.
REMEMI
a p
Japanese
in the
Portlan
until S
More than 800 peop
been imprisoned i
I feel like a spec
of the present. Hi
NOTICE
Delta Park
Vanport
City Center
Portland State University
began in Vanport.

ts
cals.
Please don't eat this fish.
GATES CLOSED AT DUSK
Yes, the "market" might be pursuing green energy. But while solutions to global warming might prove profitable, so too its ravages.
PODS are now made as 8'x8'x16' shelters, hurricane housing.
an invention motivated by reports that some victims of Hurricane Katrina slept in PODS.
"Flood control" was one argument for the Dalles Dam,
built nine years after the Columbia flooded Vanport.
many strong aromas waft this road.
Japanese Americans were ordered to bring only what they could carry. PODS (Portable On Demand Storage) are stacked here like children's blocks.
How many PODS would my possessions fill?
N FORCE AV
N MARINE DR
WARNING
Bend for meaningful conversation in loud traffic.
conversation is uncomfortable speech;
WAVE
walk
EXPO
cans were imprisoned
nter--called the
bly Center--from May
r, 1942.
Upstream the Columbia River more than 90 miles, the Dalles Dam submerges Celilo Falls, or Wyam, in backed-up waters.
"Celilo Falls sank unwillingly in the new trading/ and everyone dissolved in the fall."
--Elizabeth Woody
e
ánamo
es
help.
Bike Locker
Expo Center

Prison-Past, Flooded City

The skater glides the bend, her arm tucked behind her, speed style. She pushes through a pack of roller skaters, gripping a teammate's studded belt until she emerges in front and glides around yet another bend of the roller rink. Her teammate tangles legs with another woman, throws an elbow, and is whistled into the penalty box. Adorned with shimmering skate skirts, fake animal tails, shredded rocker t-shirts, rhinestones, glitter, and other trappings of glamor, athletes skate under names like Scratcher in the Eye, Vixen Mary, Aurora Brutalis, and Taunt-Ya Harding. A glam rocker mascot for the Guns & Rollers team spars with Nurse Ratched, mascot for the Heartless Heathers, inciting cheers from the crowd. It is another sold-out night of the Rose City roller derby at the Portland Metropolitan Exposition Center—sixty acres of buildings and parking lots at the land's edge of North Portland.

I am among the fans this autumn Saturday night, relishing the quirky theatrics that at once undermine and celebrate organized sports. During a recent block of years when I lived away from Oregon, I was lonesome for such edgy playfulness. I missed signs like "Hip Chicks Do Wine" set among railyards and industrial landscape, or the sculptural bicycles propped against rented houses, or the women's roller derby league that sells out a stadium large enough to house a small town—which it did, nearly seventy years ago.

I lived for a time in Southern Maryland, a peninsula that dangles beneath the nation's capital, and it was there that poet Lucille Clifton talked to me about slave graves in the region bearing no present-day markers. Some of the stones that previously marked the graves were re-used to build walls of local buildings, she speculated. It was during my conversations with Lucille that

I began to wonder how we might map the thickness of time and its political history. Where were all these graves Lucille urged me to remember? Beneath condominiums? Under widening swells of water? Within pastures of graves more clearly marked? If we couldn't see them, how could we remember them? The Situationists called attention to this way of reading space through graffiti during the 1968 uprisings in Paris—"Beneath the paving stones—the beach!"

Sometimes people on the East Coast would mix up where I was from—how is Seattle? they might ask—and I would believe I was preserving the secret that is Oregon, its blue-warm summer days, in the spirit of Tom McCall. "Come visit us again and again. This is a state of excitement. But for heaven's sake, don't come here to live,"[1] the former governor said in a 1971 CBS news interview, but I misremembered this story as an actual description of a road sign at the state's border with California. He was concerned with thoughtful land use in the state, and my pride in the statement shared this concern. I did not realize, though, how such a statement had been uttered at other times in our state's history with menace, and not just "don't come here to live," but also, "leave."

The area that surrounds the Portland Metropolitan Exposition Center is mostly colored green on a city map, mottled with the blue shapes of lakes and smaller bodies of water. From the vantage point of the MAX light rail stop, the landscape looks open, wide, industrial. Trucks pattern Marine Drive, north of the Expo Center, and the Columbia River is just beyond. To the south and west are wetlands, a slough where dogs run off-leash and people ride bikes, stopping to read explanatory signs about the many birds migrating in and out of the area. To the northwest is the Livestock Commerce Center, a warehouse stacked with Portable On Demand Storage Units, an asphalt company. In the northwest corner is a golf course, and southwest, a car racetrack.

There are some hints of prior inhabitants of the Expo Center. Art decorates the Max light rail stop: wind chimes clink from a structure resembling the gate of a Shinto shrine. A plaque in the Hall A lobby offers explanation. But the present moment can overwhelm the senses. The Expo Center seems all nighttime spectacle, or all daytime trade show, showcasing mobile home shows, boats shows, garden shows, and dog shows ("pretty much anything with 'show' at the end," explains an Expo Center employee).

But if we muster an imaginative memory, we can read this geography in terms of displacements and exclusions. The Portland Expo Center was constructed in the 1920s as the Pacific International Livestock Exposition Grounds, part of a larger complex of meat processing plants and stockyards along the Columbia Slough.[2] On May 5, 1942, it became the Portland Assembly Center, home to more than thirty-six hundred Japanese Americans who, one week prior, were commanded to pack belongings into suitcases—only what they could carry—register at 128 Northeast Russell Street, and affix tags to their belongings and children displaying a newly assigned family number. People quickly made whatever arrangements were possible for their land, shops, livestock, savings, evacuating farms in rural areas as well as Portland's Nihonmachi—or Japantown—a neighborhood cordoned by Burnside and Northwest Glisan, the river and Sixth Avenue, that had bustled for fifty years with apartments and laundries and hotels and photo studios and shops and medical offices and meeting houses. On May 5, 1942, Nihonmachi disappeared.[3]

When the roller derby bout ends, I walk through parking lots to catch the MAX, an area that in 1942 was the dirt ground where people lined up dressed in their hats and suits, turning their lives over to the incarceration mostly referred to as internment. In one photo, Junichi Doi sits hunched by his suitcase. On the back of the photo housed at the Oregon Historical Society, the original "Jap Camp" (scrawled in thick black pencil) has been edited with "anese,"[4] lightly penciled in. In another photograph, a boy is dressed in a wool coat with a velvet collar, his pants hiked up to show neatly folded white socks over his hightop white shoes. He rests on a chair next to a suitcase and a package wrapped in brown paper and tied with twine. The original caption in the *Oregon Journal* read, "Richard Sumida, 18 months old, chose to be comfortable while his parents arranged details of occupancy. He will have plenty of company in the assembly center."[5]

Richard Sumida and his family, as well as several thousand others, lived in partitioned spaces supplied with cots and bare bulbs suspended from wires. These residents of the Portland Assembly Center were among over one hundred thousand people imprisoned after Franklin D. Roosevelt signed Executive Order 9066 banishing Japanese Americans from the West Coast. While the army prepared its concentration camps in mostly desert regions further inland, it ordered people to live in fairgrounds, horse tracks, migrant worker camps, and here in Portland, that livestock exposition hall, where plywood was quickly laid over the dirt ground. Mae Ninomiya remembers that during those "hot summer days" she endured "the penetration of animal odors."[6]

A glance at a photograph of the Portland Assembly Center Mess Hall reveals the same old-growth wood posts[7] that today, painted black, interrupt rows of boats or campers or garden displays. People gathered for meals at the sound of a whistle, eating among thousands of clattering forks and spoons, flypaper thick with flies dangling overhead. They waited in long lines to do laundry, stacking folded clothes on newspapers spread on the floor. With canvas doors hung from rope stretched across the front of their living stalls and no roofs above their head save the steep ceiling of the massive hall, they tried to sleep among the chatter of radios and the breathing and coughing of thousands of others. Among English classes, and typhoid vaccinations, and worries of petty thievery, days passed. People married ("the wedding ceremony of Milton Maeda and Mariko Kageyama was held at Section 6") and died ("Akira Shimura's funeral was at 2:00 today") and celebrated birthdays ("This evening Nanako was invited to May Abe's birthday party") and wondered who would move where when. "The lonely days continue. I feel so exhausted and weak," Saku Tomita wrote, and then, "I was surprised to receive a beautiful and delicious cake and pie from Miss Lansfield." [8]

In those four months living in the former stockyards, residents played baseball, delivered lectures to each other about "the Nation" and "The Assembly Center Mother," romanced each other at dances, and read the *Evacuazette*, a newspaper typed out by evacuees on picnic tables. Full of social news and sports reporting, as well as information that hinted at life in future "camps," the *Evacuazette* was barred from carrying any news of World War II. The final issue reveals an optimistic tone consistent with earlier issues. In the pages of the final issue of the

Evacuazette, N. L. Bican, the Portland Asssembly Center manager, congratulates the interned for making "the Portland Assembly Center one of the most outstanding Centers on the Pacific Coast." He then urges "the same spirit of cooperation" in their "new homes" of the concentration camps, adding, "we expect you to do so."[9] By September 1942, all those interned at Portland Assembly Center had been relocated again, boarded on trains and sent to Minidoka, Idaho; Heart Mountain, Wyoming; and Tule, Lake, California; those places variously referred to as sites of "Assembly, Concentration, Detention, Evacuation, Internment, Relocation," as Lawson Inada writes in his poem, "Legends from Camp."[10]

The poet George Oppen wrote "We look back/Three hundred years and see bare land./And suffer vertigo"[11] Imagining a landscape other than a particular built environment can be challenging, but on this swathe of North Portland land, the challenge is imagining a much larger population. If we look back only sixty-six years, we are dizzied not by bare land, but the movement of people.

During those months when people were enduring life in what is now the Expo Center, a shipping tycoon named Henry Kaiser bought up the surrounding floodplain land. And as Oregon and Washington Nikkei boarded trains to inland concentration camps, crews began to build quick housing in what became known as Vanport City, two-story green buildings fitted with fourteen apartments each for workers who would build the ships to fight the war.

Those forced first into and then out of the Expo Center were blamed for the war, blamed for ancestry connecting them to a nation designated as enemy, Japan. But those who were moved into that new packed city that Henry Kaiser had built, who came from all over the nation, invited into the state because their labor promised capitalist profit—some of them descended from ancestors refused entry in Oregon. Workers who moved into Vanport helped quadruple the African American population in Oregon from 2565 in 1940 to 11,529 in 1950.[12] This small Black population in 1940 was not a quirk of history; rather, there were structural causes: Only fifteen years had passed since the state repealed from its constitution, "No free negro, or mulatto, not residing in this State at the time of the adoption of this Constitution, shall come, reside, or be within this State."[13] And about the time that racist legislation was changed in the 1920s, other national laws denied U.S. citizenship for Japanese immigrants, a population once favored for their labor when yet another group was barred from immigrating into the United States in 1882 through the Chinese Exclusion Act. Such was the cycle of racism, economic fears, and capitalist desires (and when the Japanese fell out of favor, Mexican laborers were courted).

Diked on all sides, Vanport was a sunken city, almost too low for its residents to see the sky's horizon.[14] Although spacious compared to the Portland Assembly Center, the apartments were spaced only twenty feet apart, crowding forty thousand people into the largest wartime housing project in the nation. After the war ended, the apartments were occupied by returning GIs and their families, as well as others who scraped by on a low income, and the population of the city dropped in half.

The month of May proved to be a month of upheaval on this North Portland land. While six years previously, Japanese Americans were forcibly brought to the space, during Memorial Day weekend of 1948, the new occupants were forced off the land. This time, after a winter of heavy snowfall and a warm, wet spring, the Columbia River heaved high. Early in the morning on May 30, Housing Authority of Portland employees slipped a note under the doors of Vanport apartments: "barring unforeseen developments, Vanport is safe." Late in the afternoon, though, a dike—simply a railroad trestle surrounded by dirt—broke loose, and the river smashed down on the small city as a siren wailed its warning. People climbed to the roofs of their buildings.[15]

When they moved in, residents of Vanport had been given a handbook that warned, "The apartment in which you live is very simple in its design. It is constructed of material that will not stand up unless you take care of it."[16] But the flood proved the material would not stand up, regardless. Vanport was now a lake, and the apartment buildings floated like boats on their wooden foundations. The Pacific International Livestock Exposition Grounds held its ground, an island in the sudden lake. Six years had passed since Japanese Americans were held captive, and as before internment, animals filled the quarters. Film footage shows cattle struggling to wade through the floodwater.[17]

This land—so populated before that Vanport flood—is no longer residential today. Now, in one warehouse, tons of possessions are stashed in Portable On Demand Storage containers, white boxes with blue doors, stacked box upon box upon box. Some of these boxes are now designed for people, too, people fleeing contemporary weather disasters. Citing the fact that, desperate for shelter, people lived in PODS during Hurricane Katrina, PODS vice president Tony Paalz announced the launch of Portable on Demand Shelters in 2007. "This is the solution for any disaster or catastrophic event," he said. Some say the market will correct for global warming because green energy solutions will be profitable, but the disasters are profitable, too. These 8x8x16 shelters are built to house weather refugees, contemporary counterparts of the 18,500 occupants displaced by the Vanport flood.

We might also connect the Vanport flood to further displacements that would occur nine years after Vanport was demolished, ninety miles upstream at Celilo Falls. As federal officials sought to build dams on the Columbia River, they argued for irrigation water and cheap electricity. It was a third argument, though, that gained emotional heft from the Vanport flood—that dams could provide flood control.[18] Despite more than twelve thousand years of Native gathering and fishing at the Celilo Falls,[19] and despite treaty rights that promised "the right of taking fish, at all usual and accustomed grounds and stations,"[20] Dalles Dam was built. On March 10, 1957, the massive gates of the newly constructed Dalles Dam closed, and six hours later, Celilo Falls (or Wyam in Kiksht and Ichishkiin) was smothered in raised and backed-up water.[21] "Celilo Falls sank unwillingly in the new trading/ and everyone dissolved in the fall," wrote Elizabeth Woody in the poem "She-Who-Watches, The Names are Prayer."[22] Not only were the people of the original Celilo Falls village displaced, but also, thousands of years of spiritual and cultural practices. Where the river is calm, it once crashed in waterfalls. Where there is a dam, there were once dipnet fishers.

I can see the Columbia River from a boat dock off Marine Drive where houseboats bob. I know that some of the people who traded at Celilo Falls must have passed over this very land. Maps show indigenous Chinookan language speakers in the North Portland area. If we look back 300 years, 200 years, the land is not bare.

At the time of the flood in 1948, a quarter of the Vanport residents were African American. Japanese Americans comprised a smaller resident population of nine hundred people, according to one *Oregonian* account.[23] Many returned to few possessions when they were released from the internment camps, their previous housing now lost to them. Some sought the low income housing of Vanport, returning by economic necessity to the site where they had been forcibly moved before. Their recent lives were characterized by upheaval—first, as incarceration, then, economic desperation, and now, a flood.

One such person was Sadao Mizuno. A photographer, he once ran Rose City Photo Studio in his Nihonmachi apartment, snapping portraits. After relocation to the Portland Assembly Center, he was sent to the Minidoka internment camp, where he continued to make art. Upon release, though, he had no home to return to—Nihonmachi was gone. He ended up at Vanport. In a photograph, he stands before a door to what looks like a storage facility at Vanport, his white hair combed forward. He sports a trimmed goatee and wire glasses, and wears a baggy suit, his left thumb tucked into a pocket of a sweater vest.[24]

When the flood came, so the story goes,[25] the seventy-five-year-old photographer said he had been moved too many times. This time, given a choice, he did not move again—and he died in the Vanport flood,[26] one of the fifteen documented dead, among many others who were never found.

In a poem, Bertolt Brecht described holding fishing tackle from a second-hand store and imagining that it "Was left behind by those Japanese fishermen/ Whom they have now driven from the West Coast into camps/As suspect aliens; that it came into my hands/ To keep me in mind of so many/Unsolved but not insoluble/Questions of humanity."[27] A poetic imagination can be an insistent one, comfortable enough in uncertainties to demand meaning. We cannot easily see a history of displacement in the parking lots, roller derby bouts, and wet-green terrain of the land that abuts the Columbia River. Such awareness must be deeply felt, though, as immigrant labor continues to be regarded and discarded as a means to profit. Such awareness must be deeply felt while the U.S. government incarcerates so many people in prisons across the nation as well as remote to its borders. In the ambiguity that is the present, we easily consent to practices that are distant, or cloaked, or difficult to interpret, as we have many times before.

It is now late winter as I walk the paths of that wet-green land, cooler than the day of the Vanport flood, but the sky is as blue as it would have been then. Canadian geese flock in the sky. A Great Blue Heron swoops toward the slough. People gather at the Portland

International Raceway for car racing, but the entire area is much less populated than it was when Japanese Americans were interned in the Expo Center, which I can see across the slough. It is much less populated than when Vanport was the second-largest city in Oregon. It is much less populated than when, for one hundred days in 1959, the Oregon Centennial Exposition briefly claimed the land. During that celebratory fair and trade show, a "Japan Trade Center" showcased Japanese goods in the same space where Japanese Americans were held captive less than two decades prior. A miniature dam was on display for wonderment, two years after a dam destroyed Celilo Falls. A landscaped show called "The International Garden of Tomorrow" drew spectators on the land where children would have wandered their Vanport City neighborhoods.[28]

Today, as I walk along the land, a breeze reminding me of the water nearby, I am hard-pressed to see any of that history. One man collects bottles from this moist earth, I read in a local newspaper, constructing a glass memoir of the prior inhabitants (these are the crèmes they used, these are the pickles, this is the shoe polish, milk, liquor), [29] his attempt at reading this history. I watch as buses shuttle people from the Expo Center parking lot to the Portland International Raceway, which was first built on the ruins of Vanport roads. Do we need our ruins visible? How much can we experience the past through interpretative signs? I carry old maps, but sometimes the space seems illegible because reclaimed wetlands and construction changed the shape of the land. I cross-check books and oral histories and photographs. I imagine. The birds and race-cars and boat shows and roller derby bouts. The blue-doored, white blocks heavy with possessions. The prison-past, the flooded city.

notes

1. Brent Walth. *Fire at Eden's Gate.* Portland: Oregon Historical Press, 1998, pp. 313-314.
2. "Expo History." Accessed Dec 8, 2006. <www.expocenter.org/history.htm>.
3. George Katagiri, Cannon Kitayama, and Liz Nakazawa. *Nihonmachi: Portland's Japantown Remembered.* Portland: Oregon Nikkei Legacy Center, 2002.
4. Photo of Junichi Doi is in the Portland Assembly Center Vertical File. Oregon Historical Society.
5. Portland Assembly Center Vertical File. Oregon Historical Society.
6. Mae Ninomiya. Oral History. History of Kenton. Kenton Neighborhood Assocation. Accessed Jan. 8, 2008 <cchr.org/comm./slough/oral/mninomiya.htm>.
7. Portland Assembly Center Vertical File. Oregon Historical Society.
8. All quotations in this paragraph are from "Portland Assembly Center: Diary of Saku Tomita," courtesy of the Oregon Historical Society Research Library, Saku Tomita collection, MSS 1482, translated by Zuigaku Kodachi and Jan Heikkala, edited by Janet Cormack. Reproduced in part from *Oregon Historical Quarterly*, Summer, 1980, pp.149-171. <ccrh.org/comm/slough/primary/diary.htm>.
9. *Evacuazette: Farewell Edition.* Portland Assembly Center. Vol II: No. 4, August 25, 1942. Oregon Historical Society Archives. I retrieved other issues of the Evacuazette from the Densho archive <www.densho.org>. James Hirabayashi discusses the accuracy of the term "concentration camp" in his article "'Concentration Camp'or 'Relocation Center': What's in a Name?" originally published in the *Japanese American National Museum Quarterly* (Vol. 9, No. 3, 1994), and reprinted online <www.discovernikkei.org/en/journal/2008/4/24/enduring-communities/>. Franklin Delano Roosevelt himself used the term "concentration camps" in a 1944 press conference, as did Harold Ickes, Secretary of Interior, in 1946.
10. Lawson Inada. *Legends from Camp.* Minneapolis: Coffee House Press, 1992.
11. George Oppen. "The Building of the Skyscraper." *Collected Poems.* NY: New Directions, 1975, p. 131.
12. "States of Origin of African American Residents of Vanport," Statistics compiled from U.S. Bureau of Census, 1850-1990. Center for Columbia River History. Accessed January 10, 2008, <ccrh.org/comm/slough/primary/afamstats.htm>.
13. *Constitution of the State of Oregon.* <ccrh.org/comm/slough/primary/orgconst.htm>. While few African Americans settled in Oregon in the late nineteenth century, some did under tremendous difficulty. George Washington Cochran was born a slave in Virginia. He and his family moved west until they arrived in Oregon, hoping to find greater freedoms, but they faced laws barring settlement. Cochran's parents were white—they adopted him as a child—so they bought property and transferred it to Cochran so he could realize his plan for a city. He founded Centralia, Washington.
14. Manly Mabel. *Vanport.* Portland: Oregon Historical Press, p. 31.

15 Manly Mabel. *Vanport.* Portland: Oregon Historical Press, p.105.

16 *Vanport Handbook.* Original document in the Oregon Historical Society Collections. Accessed January 10, 2008 <ccrh.org/comm/slough/primary/rules.htm>.

17 "Vanport Flood." Moving Image #01172, Oregon Historical Society Collections.

18 The statement from Tony Paalz, who at the time was vice-president of PODS, was reported on WTVT Fox 13 in Tampa, Florida on July 13, 2007.The background on the arguments for damming the Columbia River at Celilo Falls are in Katrine Barber's *Death of Celilo Falls* (Seattle: University of Washington Press, 2005, p. 34).

19 Elizabeth Woody. "Wyam,: Echo of Falling Water." *Seven Hands, Seven Hearts*, Portland: The Eighth Mountain Press, 1994, p. 63.

20 Joseph Cone and Sandy Ridlington, eds. "Stevens Treaty Negotiations." *The Northwest Salmon Crisis: A Documentary History*, Corvallis: Oregon State University Press, p. 178

21 Elizabeth Woody. "Wyam: Echo of Falling Water." *Seven Hands, Seven Hearts*, Portland: The Eighth Mountain Press, 1994, p. 64.

22 Elizabeth Woody. "She-Who-Watches, The Names are Prayer." *Seven Hands, Seven Hearts*, Portland: The Eighth Mountain Press, 1994, pp. 76-77.

23 Sura Rubenstein. "May 30, 1948 Flood of Change." *Oregonian.* May 24, 1998, p. M01, Sunrise Edition.

24 Photo of Sadao Mizuno. Oregon Nikkei Legacy Center Archives, #373.

25 Conversation with Rebecca Patchett. Collections Manager. Oregon Nikkei Legacy Center, January 9, 2008.

26 "The Dead the Anniversary." *Oregonian*, May 24, 1998, M05, Sunrise Edition.

27 Bertolt Brecht. "The Fishing Tackle." *Poems: 1913-1956.* NY: Methuen, 1976, p. 386.

28 Larry McCarten. "It's a Big Show—Weird, Exotic, Amazing." *Oregon Journal.* June 9, 1959, 19S.

29 Jennifer Anderson. "Time in a Bottle." *Portland Tribune.* February 1, 2008, A1.

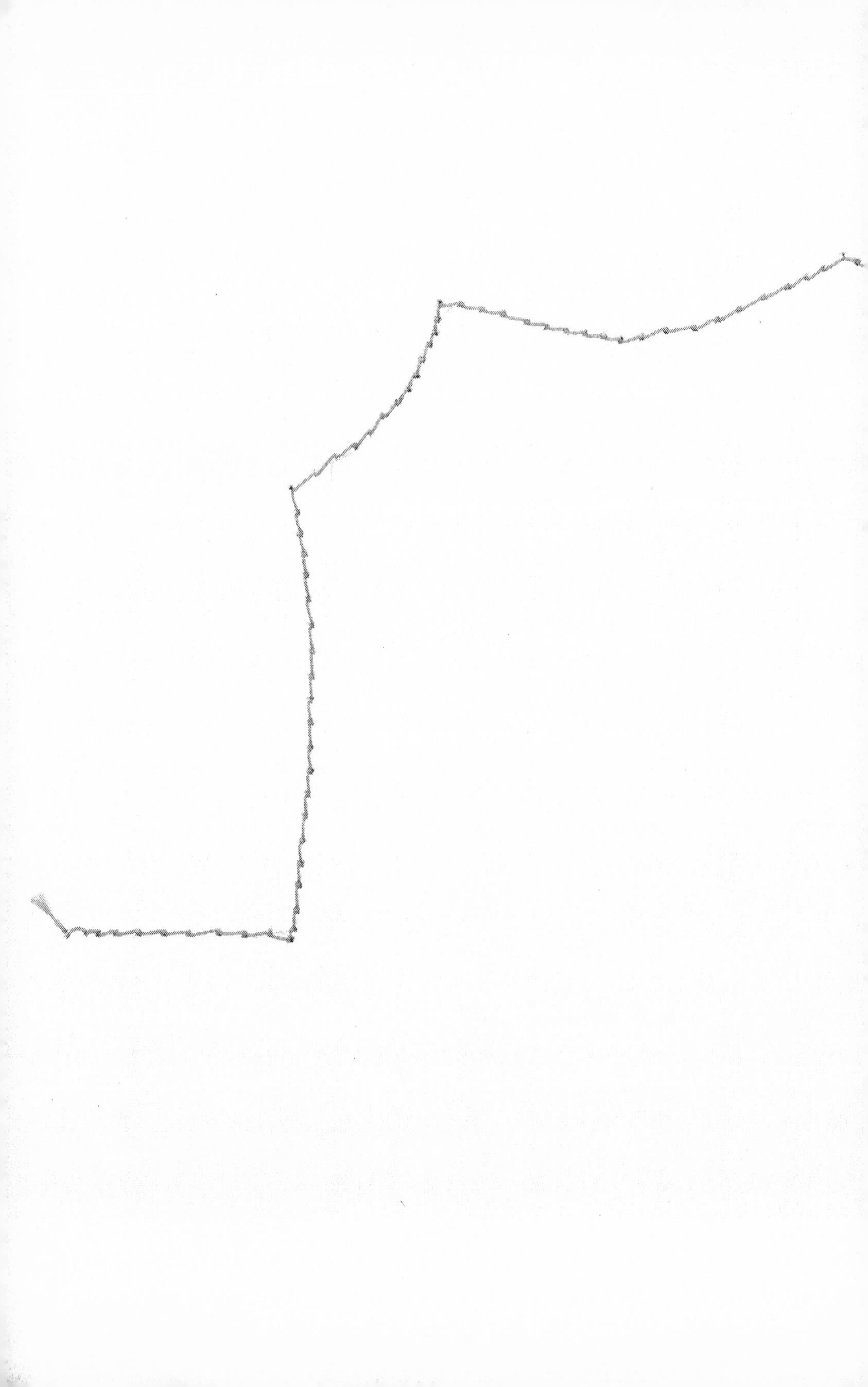

To arrive at this poem, please fly to Portland International Airport (airport code PDX) and board a MAX light-rail train to the Rose Garden. Transfer to a northbound Yellow Line train and travel to the end of the line, Expo Center.

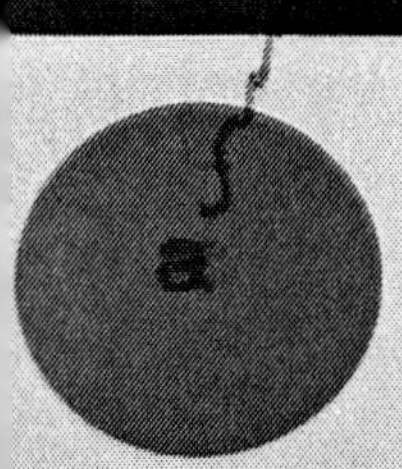

Alternatively, please travel to the Portland Amtrak Station, then walk to the Old Town/Chinatown MAX stop, site of the former Nihonmachi, or Japantown, which disappeared in May 1942 when all residents were forcibly evacuated to the Portland Assembly Center, or Expo Center. Board the Yellow Line, northbound train to the end of the line.

Here, this poem begins.

生くる身に解せぬ事多く夏星光る

For the living
many incomprehensible incidents
summer stars shine
  -Shizuku Uyemaruko

Perhaps you might jot down sounds &
scents as you walk?

Or maybe other perceptions? Taste? Sight? Touch?
Movement? Bodily Discomforts? Temperature & other
marks of weather? Weather-vane arrows? Vertigo?
Memories? Inattentions? Questions? Curios of thought?
Assorted intuitions?

An ode by accretion.

elsewhere erstwhile

here in this time

there are so many

of us on this planet

USER TO SUPPLY LOCK. Prisoner to supply shackles. Barbed wire. Dog to supply leash. Convicted to supply stenographer. Citizen to supply amnesia. Child to supply carbon emissions. Fish to supply lure. Chickens to supply fox. Raccoon. Eggs to supply oppossum. Citizen to supply amnesia. Citizen to supply personal electronic devices. Headache to supply exhaust. City to supply benzene. Herons to supply PCB. Tenement to supply flood. Prisoner to supply censor. Dipnetters to supply dam. Citizen, user, taker, sweetheart, raccoon. Come. Take good care. Let's walk.

Bike
Locke
• 24 hour use
• User to supply loc
• For bike storage o
TRIMET

PORTLAND EXPOSITION
DIABETIC DAY THURS
RC GUN & KNIFE
FRI 12 SAT &
RC CAT SHOW
SAT & SUN 10
MODEL HORSE SHOW

Event Calendar / September through April / Portland Fall RV & Van Show / Design-2-Part Show / Rose City Rollers--Roller Derby / Hardy Plant Society of Oregon Garden Fair / Northwest Quilting Expo / Portland Regional Gem & Mineral Show Association / Silver Collector Car Auction / Portland Fall Home & Garden Show / NWCCA Car Show & Swap Meet / Rip City Cats / Food Services of America Annual Food / Woodworking Show / America's Largest Antique & Collectible Show / Catlin Gabel School Rummage Sale / Girl Fest / Portland Metro RV Dealers present the Fall RV Show of Shows / Portland Concrete Show / NW Knockdown--Roller Derby Flat Track Natl. Championships / Portland Skifever and Snowboard Show / Portland Reptile Show & Sale / Rose City Gun & Knife Show / America's Largest Christmas Bazaar / Rose City Gun & Knife Show / Portland Boat Show / Oregon State Marine Board / Rose City Classic Dog Show / Celebrate! Portland (scrapbooking) / Oregon Cats, Inc. / Pacific Northwest Sportsmen's Show & Sport Fishing

b

Boat Show / Portland Rod & Custom Show / The Great Train Expo / Home Builders Assoc. of Metro Portland--Board Meeting / Pro Start State High School Culinary Championships / America's Largest Antique & Collectible Show / Heirloom's Portland Rubber Stamp & Paper Arts Festival / Portland's Largest Garage Sale

named
in a word
or so

wave or touch
knuckle-to-
knuckle

your self-
writing

dare I
declare

a bit
of swagger

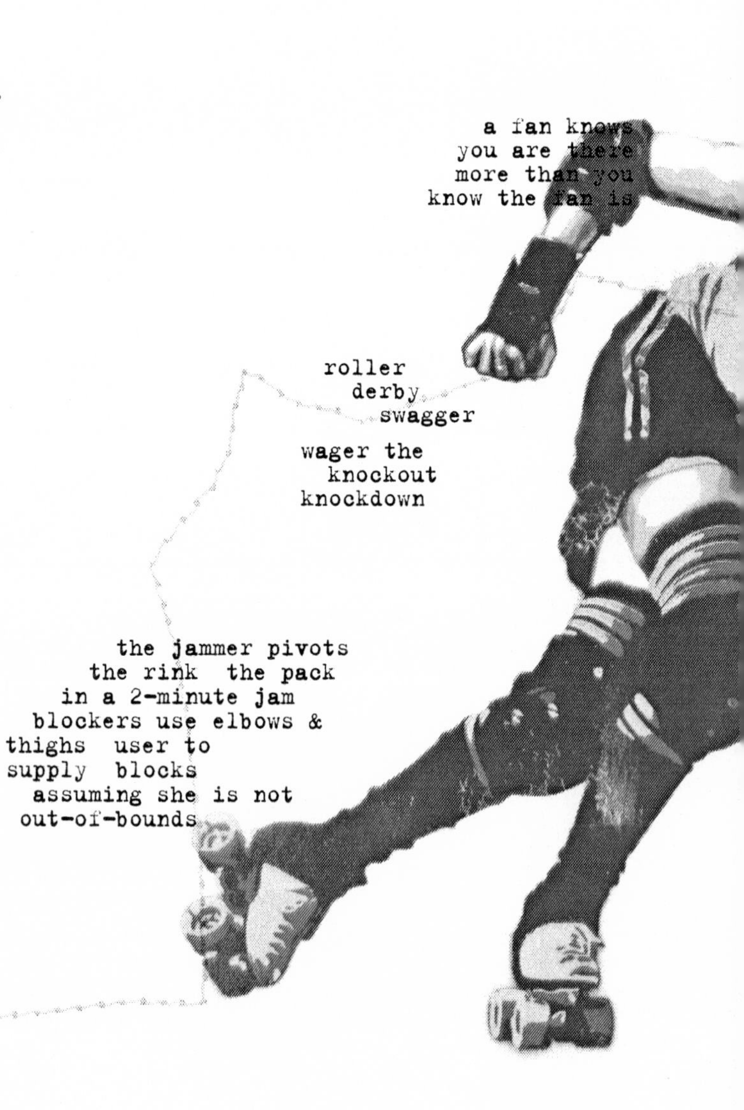

a bit wager
--so many
of us afoot

a fan knows
you are there
more than you
know the fan is

roller
derby
swagger

wager the
knockout
knockdown

the jammer pivots
the rink the pack
in a 2-minute jam
blockers use elbows &
thighs user to
supply blocks
assuming she is not
out-of-bounds

Autographs

WFTDA
HARLEY RAFFLE
TONIGHT @ 8
GRAB YOUR TICKETS
NOW!!!
ROSE CITY
Rollers
a game of brutal beauty
"The Rose City Rollers are women of attitude, passion and athleticism playing a hard-hitting sport of speed and skill. They were pioneers in the rebirth of roller derby and continue to foster its growth. Their goals are to serve their community by empowering women, providing entertainment for their fans and supporting charitable causes."
Honey Hellfire
Minnie VanMayhem
Cher the Pain x10
Slambo
Shove Me Tender #51
Fist O'Fury
Sully Skullkicker
Skintastic Dynamite #308
Butcher Block 97
Kickassedy plays derby.
Hard Knox
Smack Ya Sideways
Sulfuric Acid

named in a word or so
now I know you were here (are where?)
erstwhile

hello baby boy Shimizu born July 6, 1942, 8:42 PM, 7 pounds 7 ounces; hello baby girl Onichi, July 10, 1942, 9:08 AM (no weight reported); hello baby boy Yoshihara, July 21, 1942, 2:54 PM, 6 pounds 2 ounces; hello baby boy Kawamoto, July 21, 1942, 10:03 PM, 6 pounds 5 ounces; hello baby boy Okamoto, August 15, 1942, 7:20 PM, 7 pounds 12 ounces

hello Boy Scout Troop 123, Explorer Troop 623

hello 'new arrivals,' 'evacuees,' 'colonists'; hello Chain Gang Baseball Team, hello Kats Nakayama, homerun hitter & electrician foreman

hello Albert Oyama, ping pong champion, Hito 'Heat' Heyamoto, Jumbo Murakami, grandslammer
the Old Timers, the Bachelors, the Farmers, the Townies,
the Dishwashers, the Fujii baseball teams
the Wapato Wolves & Country Sister softball teams

hello first aid givers, talent show emcees, chicken pox sufferers, diphtheria immunizers, calisthenics teachers, cake bakers, kindergarten teachers, model airplane builders, chatty neighbors

hello Zombie day dancers, sugar beet pickers
Issei, Nisei, Sansei leaders

hello. hello. hello

hello Midora Baker, separated from your parents, carceral childhood, sixty years later and I worry about you

hello Akira Shimura 6 years old & dead on July 10, 1942

hello to the cook on break in the sun 'too near' the fence, suddenly shot by guards, the blood on your white coat another man remembers, wondering what happened, so do I

hello to the journalist watching the Jantzen Beach ferris wheel lights from the Evacuazette balcony, 'knowing that is outside,' hello Sunday visitors speaking at the barbed fence

hello Michi Yasunaga & James Wakagawa betrothed June 29, 1942

hello Madame Fifi Suzette, talent show impresario, hello Chiseo Shoji, cartooning the flyswatters, the toe-stompers, the clog-clompers

bound for Minidoka, Heart Mountain

hello Rose Katagiri, Evacuazette typist bound for Tule Lake June 10 1942, the Katagiri family & Akagis & Moriokas & Yamaguchis & Watanabes bound for Tule Lake, bound, carceral

there are so many of us on this planet

carceral & elsewhere, some 300 miles south by new highways, Tule Lake
a land still strung with barbed wire
near petroglyphs where recently & anciently Modoc people
peopled the land

hello Clara Yokota, your name written in stone
now I know you were there (are where?)
named in a word or so
hello Betty Yamashiro
there are so many of us on this planet
                    some at Tule Lake, 1942 43 44 45 1946
                    some who said 'no' and then 'no' to 'loyalty' oaths
                    imperiled, one has refusal
                      : hunger, to strike with
                      : a name, to withhold   or utter, an autograph
                                                a tag in stone
                                                personal effects

BETTY YAMASHIRO

elsewhere, ninety miles upstream, the river is
grand in its gorge where inside is Celilo, now
fifty years past its smothering, Dalles Dam
backing up the river over the waterfall

where millennia of people gathered, dipnets
& trading, where now people are gathering,
demanding the dam be breached, and a boy stands
near railroad tracks near the river, and he
conjures answers and grandness. what else do
you need

to know, he asks. when your hand reaches for
food among others, he answers, take back

your hand if another is wrinkled. wait. what
else can I tell you? sturgeon are in that river,
old and low in holes. as the light lessons

swells of people feast. I take my seat near a
pear orchardist, this is his transition year of
loneliness, every year

a transition, lonely toward so much knowledge,
as if I could remember dipnets & trading

without memory. I try

in this gorge, light with old ice, salmon
rights & new lights in the city in which I live.

elsewhere, ninety miles downstream & then
upstream another river more miles at the Rose
Garden arena in the city where I live & write
by light

made by the river & its losses, a man holds
a sturgeon caught in the near & toxic river,
its side slit & red gills flashing. the man
with the fish

talks to a man scalping tickets to a Rod
Stewart concert, each recalling

fishing at one dam or another as boys, a walk

light flashing near them, Celilo a dammed-up
waterfall more than 90 miles upstream.

in a landscape, a business park

in a landscape, a business park is a paraphrase, a summary of a glance. I rarely notice the occupants. Stockyard Commerce Center. Animals present? Beyond our view, beyond grass green as turf landscaped for our pleasure. "There is a whole lot of joy in eating Sara Lee bakery, deli and sweet goods, and we hope every bit of joy finds you" because "Nobody doesn't like Sara Lee." Wooing language worked into brand identity. Branded. Animals present? Once I met a woman flushed with red, burned not from the sun but from a weekend of branding. Burns, Oregon.

FNTG National Records Centers. "We understand that in today's business environment access to critical information is an advantage."

Expeditors International. "Our logistics solutions touch on all aspects of the supply chain."

Mission Focus. "Mission Foodservice tortillas are for the culinary curious."

WESTERN DEFENSE COMMAND AND FOURTH ARMY
WARTIME CIVIL CONTROL ADMINISTRATION

civil control

civil

Presidio of San Francisco, California

control

May 6, 1942

INSTRUCTIONS TO ALL PERSONS OF JAPANESE ANCESTRY

with sufficient

Living in the Following Area:

All of the County of Clackamas, State of Oregon, and all of that portion of the County of Multnomah, State of Oregon, east of the west side of 122nd Avenue and the extension thereof, from the northern limits of the said county to the southern limits of said county.

exclusion

Pursuant to the provisions of Civilian Exclusion Order No. 46, this Headquarters, dated May 6, 1942, all persons of Japanese ancestry, both alien and non-alien, will be evacuated from the above area by 12 o'clock noon, P. W. T., Tuesday, May 12, 1942.

No Japanese person living in the above area will be permitted to change residence after 12 o'clock noon, P. W. T., Wednesday, May 6, 1942, without obtaining special permission from the representative of the Commanding General, Northwestern Sector, at the Civil Control Station located at:

civil control

Administration Building,
Gresham Fair Grounds,
Gresham, Oregon.

Such permits will only be granted for the purpose of uniting members of a family, or in cases of grave emergency.

The Civil Control Station is equipped to assist the Japanese population affected by this evacuation in the following ways: civil control

1. Give advice and instructions on the evacuation.
2. Provide services with respect to the management, leasing, sale, storage or other disposition of most kinds of property, such as real estate, business and professional equipment, household goods, boats, automobiles and livestock.
3. Provide temporary residence elsewhere for all Japanese in family groups.
4. Transport persons and a limited amount of clothing and equipment to their new residence.

transport persons elsewhere

The Following Instructions Must Be Observed:

1. A responsible member of each family, preferably the head of the family, or the person in whose name most of the property is held, and each individual living alone, will report to the Civil Control Station to receive further instructions. This must be done between 8:00 A. M. and 5:00 P. M. on Thursday, May 7, 1942, or between 8:00 A. M. and 5:00 P. M. on Friday, May 8, 1942. each member of the family
2. Evacuees must carry with them on departure for the Assembly Center, the following property:
   (a) Bedding and linens (no mattress) for each member of the family; plainly marked
   (b) Toilet articles for each member of the family;
   (c) Extra clothing for each member of the family;
   (d) Sufficient knives, forks, spoons, plates, bowls and cups for each member of the family;
   (e) Essential personal effects for each member of the family. personal effects

   All items carried will be securely packaged, tied and plainly marked with the name of the owner and numbered in accordance with instructions obtained at the Civil Control Station. The size and number of packages is limited to that which can be carried by the individual or family group. of the living
3. No pets of any kind will be permitted.
4. No personal items and no household goods will be shipped to the Assembly Center.
5. The United States Government through its agencies will provide for the storage, at the sole risk of the owner, of the more substantial household items, such as iceboxes, washing machines, pianos and other heavy furniture. Cooking utensils and other small items will be accepted for storage if crated, packed and plainly marked with the name and address of the owner. Only one name and address will be used by a given family.
6. Each family, and individual living alone, will be furnished transportation to the Assembly Center or will be authorized to travel by private automobile in a supervised group. All instructions pertaining to the movement will be obtained at the Civil Control Station. that which can be carried

Go to the Civil Control Station between the hours of 8:00 A. M. and 5:00 P. M., Thursday, May 7, 1942, or between the hours of 8:00 A. M. and 5:00 P. M., Friday, May 8, 1942, to receive further instructions.

J. L. DeWITT
Lieutenant General, U. S. Army
Commanding

SEE CIVILIAN EXCLUSION ORDER NO. 46

The size and number of packages is limited to that which can be carried by the individual or family group No pets of any kind will be permitted No personal items and no household goods will be shipped to the Assembly Center

e

Innovation drives your satisfaction
PODS transformed the hassle and headaches of moving and storage with a steadfast commitment to innovation. The commitment has forever changed the moving and storage experience for thousands of PODS customers.

The revolutionary PODS storage container
PODS revolutionized the moving and storage industry by introducing the concept of portable storage containers--a storage unit that is brought to you. With PODS, you can pack at your leisure or we can arrange for a team of professional packers--then move your storage container when you are ready. Weather-resistant, PODS containers offer ground level loading making the packing process easy and safe.

PODS Container Fast Facts
Sizes: Containers are approximately 8x7x7, 8x8x12, and 8x8x16
Materials: Steel frame construction with a marine grade wood interior and aluminum skin exterior
Weight: Empty weight is approximately 2,500 lbs (8x8x16)
Capacity: 7,500 lbs of material (8x8x16)
Durability: Able to withstand a wind velocity of 110 miles per hour when partially filled.
Our patented lift and transport system--The PODZILLA
PODS delivery trucks are equipped with a patented hydraulic lift system, PODZILLA, designed to reduce any shifting of contents. It securely transports the PODS container to and from your locations and to our Storage Centers.

How many PODS would my purchases pack

if my purchases could pack more than a sack?

My purchases would pack all the PODS in the stack

when I purchase all the products I track

What a relief. Portable On Demand Shelter, when you need it most. We have no control over mother nature, but we can be prepared. Our unique Portable On Demand Shelter (TM) provides temporary housing to citizens in need and offers first reponders and emergency workers a place to stay close to impacted areas. This highly specialized container is ready to occupy and complete with : * Air Conditioner and heat *Toilet and shower facilities * Sleeping area for 5 people * Cooking facilities The Portable On Demand Shelter can support up to 5 people. With the generator and power hookup, it requires minimal preparation and is ready to be put in service minutes after delivery. This specialized container was built with formaldehyde - free materials and can significantly reduce the cost of temporary housing. PODS(R) is dedicated to helping those in need. Our specialized emergency response containers are delivered by our unique PODZILLA(R) lift system and supported by our state-of-the-art deployment system servicing 47 states and Australia and Canada.

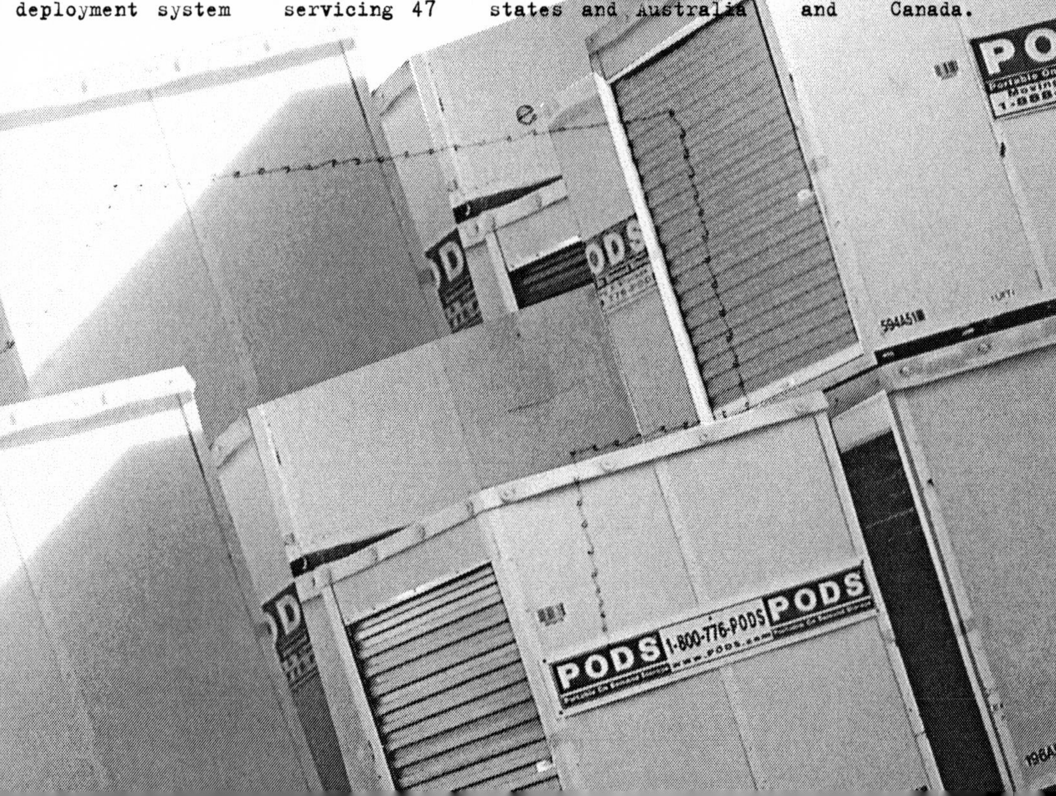

rules & regulations
you live

RESIDE

any alterations
are not allowed

HANDBO

in emergency

you take care

This Resident Handbook has been compiled for your information.
If you keep it readily accessible, it may prove helpful in time of emergency.
THE FOLLOWING RULE & REGULATIONS ARE A PART OF YOUR LEASE
APARTMENTS: The apartment in which you live is very simple in its design.
It is constructed of material that will not stand up unless you take care of it.
ALTERATIONS: Any attempted alterations would result in serious damage to the apartment.
alterations, therefore, are not allowed.

you take
care

take
care

take care

VANPO

you take care

OUSING AUTHORITY OF PORT

rules &

take care

ST

OK

RT

D, OREGON

the walkway
to a home
is trespass
when a home
is a squat
'to pass beyond or across'

flâneur with a conscience, trespasser on a payroll, my
brother leads me beyond the gate,
down the once-road brushed with
grasses & briars & I wor-
ry about who owns what
& where I can be, but
he coaxes forth our
coastal knowledge,
the Oregon beaches
where who owns
what is not such a
concern among wet
sand, driftwood,
dry sand, beach
grasses. these are
not Hollywood Beaches,
these are night beaches lit
with bonfires. people
trusted with fire
beyond my trust. family
lore--a fire burned
through Umpqua Valley &
my grandfather, the water
witcher, laid flat in a
hole covered with a wet
blanket the fire would
not pass. one week
prior my father, a
boy, had sold his
prized cow at a
fair, & it was,
that 'carried'
the family for-
ward. there's
more to the
lore. the horse
that outraced
the fire. prop-
erty burns. I
walk many pre-
scribed roads,
but here my
brother
points to
a ruined
shelter,
not a
squat, it
seems, no
trappings
of human
eating &
sleeping

WAYS TO REDUCE EXPOSURE TO PCBs FROM EATING FISH

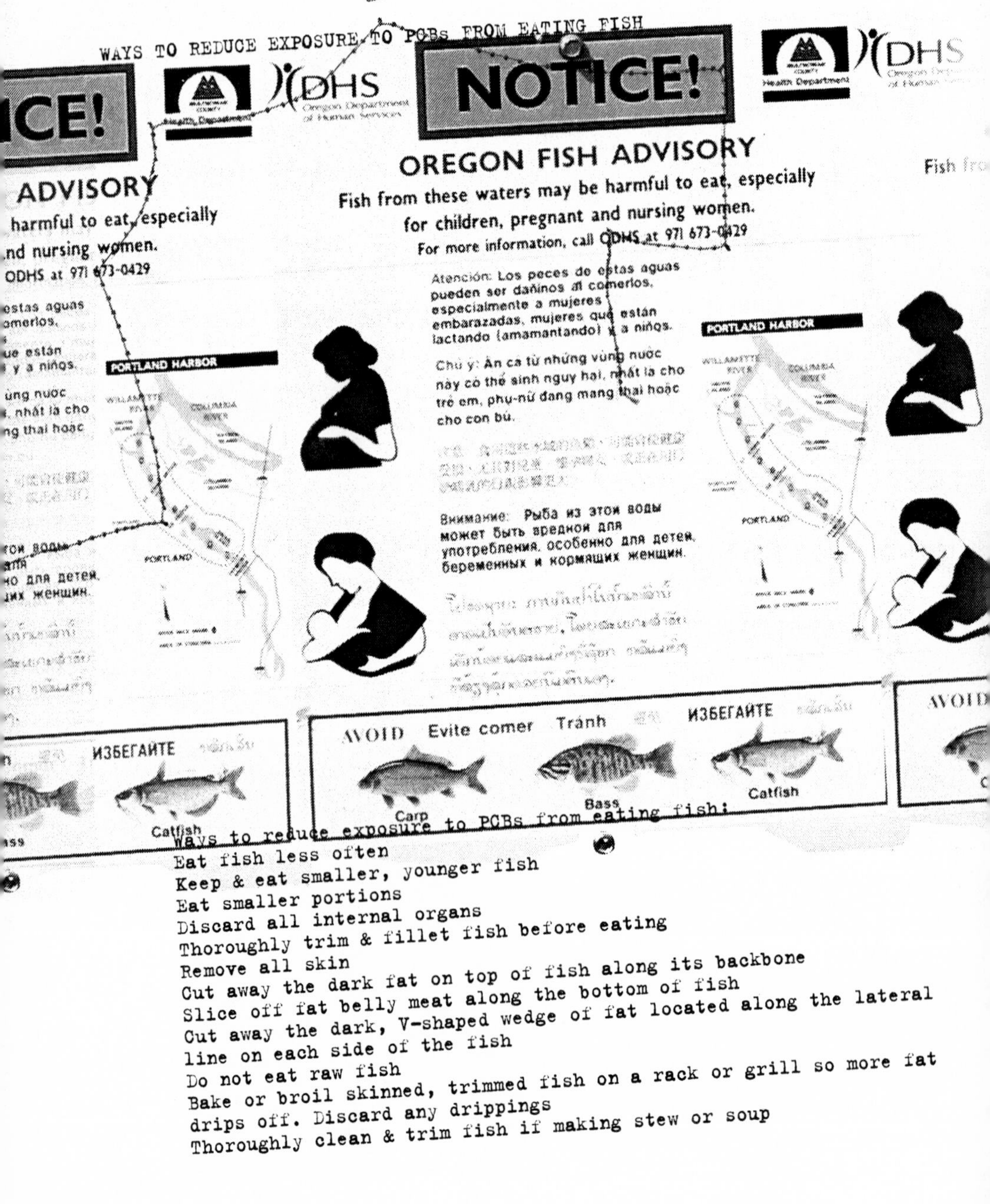

NOTICE!
DHS
Oregon Department of Human Services
Health Department
OREGON FISH ADVISORY
Fish from these waters may be harmful to eat, especially for children, pregnant and nursing women.
For more information, call ODHS at 971 673-0429
Atención: Los peces de estas aguas pueden ser dañinos al comerlos, especialmente a mujeres embarazadas, mujeres que están lactando (amamantando) y a niños.
Chú ý: Ăn cá từ những vùng nước này có thể sinh nguy hại, nhất là cho trẻ em, phụ-nữ đang mang thai hoặc cho con bú.
Внимание: Рыба из этой воды может быть вредной для употребления, особенно для детей, беременных и кормящих женщин.
PORTLAND HARBOR
WILLAMETTE RIVER
COLUMBIA RIVER
PORTLAND
AVOID Evite comer Tránh ИЗБЕГАЙТЕ
Carp
Bass
Catfish

Ways to reduce exposure to PCBs from eating fish:

Eat fish less often
Keep & eat smaller, younger fish
Eat smaller portions
Discard all internal organs
Thoroughly trim & fillet fish before eating
Remove all skin
Cut away the dark fat on top of fish along its backbone
Slice off fat belly meat along the bottom of fish
Cut away the dark, V-shaped wedge of fat located along the lateral line on each side of the fish
Do not eat raw fish
Bake or broil skinned, trimmed fish on a rack or grill so more fat drips off. Discard any drippings
Thoroughly clean & trim fish if making stew or soup

gates closed at dusk
a rabbit brushes scorched brambles

cars are parked, someone's lost
a business park is elsewhere

finance tenders its dodgy trust
so much sharing soaked in sludge

bass & catfish ingest the mess
a rustle mixed with a motored roar

someone up & dies regardless
of the company, life's quiet again

stone piles shiver toward dust
the beloved's zest through haze

water records a chemical trust
golf-calm among a race-car swell

surrounding a seed, a paper husk
someone is very wealthy today

the sky rippling with airplane violence
someone with friends in charge

a slough is slow under a heron's watch
an idle engine still quivers with work

that levy breeched, someone's lost
the ticketbooth is slow & wide

a dragonfly on a dry leaf, quivering
with work, life's quiet again

Notice a gravel lot, a ticket booth
or security station in its northwest
corner. Walk toward the roar of
racecars among trees, and notice stone
ruins, stairs that lead to a sunken
amphitheater. Who were its masons? Are
these ruins of Vanport? Efforts of the
WPA? Beyond the amphitheater, a mud
slough, perhaps some ducks in sudden
flight. Standing on this stage, its
backdrop tagged in green bubble letters,
you might compose an ode, choose
language to speak of this place.

Here are words other walkers uttered,
collaboratively improvised on September
28, 2008. I misheard much, rearranged
some, but mostly tried to 'get it down.'

MUD SLOUGH ODE

vaguely expected silence of a vacant parking spot
river   & salt   & shed snakeskin   & a lone brown duck
RESERVED FOR WHITE MARINE   desolation preserved in thoroughfare

disfruta el sabor   shadows of dragonflies on the lost garden
rhythm   & green scum   & planes   & fish advisory
SEAL COAT CARBON SEAL   acorns cracking underfoot

animals captive water captive   I smell something   PCB?
leaky ovens   & free cement   airplanes possibly heading for Japan
commerce rattles   intermittent drones   heron-like missiles

a white mailbox   sewage and/ or coyote manure   commerce
sweetness of the sewage   harsh investment properties
commerce   expectancy of a parking spot

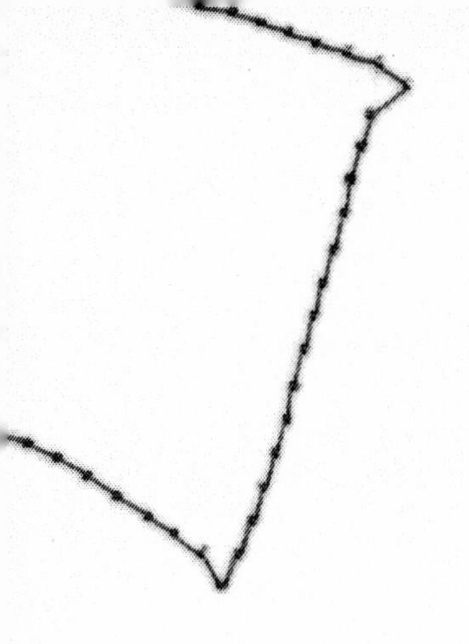

cars & trucks lined the shut-off road

cars & trucks lined the shut-off road, folks lounging
in lawn chairs as they might at a tailgating party,
racecars braced on trailers.

one night at the Vanport MAX stop

one night at the Vanport MAX stop, transit employees converged with their cameras. Past dusk, the sky was dark blue, the moon, orange-red. The men & women aimed their cameras at the shelter roof, which was quilted with hundreds of spider webs, spiders rapidly spinning more.

a note on the language of this poetic investigation

Much of my extended family migrated to Oregon within the last century—for some, they came to find the "Land of Milk and Honey," as one brochure beckoned; for others, love relations tugged them in; and for others, logging. They settled in the Umpqua Valley and the Willamette Valley, where I grew up. Family netted together in Oregon, and a variegated identity formed around the place—its forests, ocean, mountains. I recall a childhood of writing in sand, reading on boulders, climbing trees, skiing cross-country. A country cemetery with coffins wedged deep between old growth cedars. A dock where crabs boiled in a fire-pit pot. Alleys and rooftops and underground tunnels in the small city where I grew up.

Some ancestors spoke Swedish and Norwegian and Irish in the last century, but I have inherited English, and it is through English and my particular history that I investigate this place and its histories. I pull in only small bits of other languages significant to these histories, pronouncing the Japanese of haiku written in internment camps.

I have married a man whose family came more recently to Oregon, who speaks to me about this place in English but also speaks Spanish, whose ancestors are Ukrainian and German. Our family has extended in new ways, netting in indigenous ties to this place: Our daughter's ancestors lived near the Columbia River, but far upstream from North Portland, and spoke a language, Ichishkiin, also called Sahaptin. Never has the "English-only" debate seemed stranger than when I think of languages like Ichishkiin and Kiksht, words and rhythms born and cultivated and shared here. English is an imperial language in this land, a vocabulary built from other trees, other weathers, other animals. We change it, adding words and sounds and patterns—I am told that Oregon English involves a hiss, the sss sound a microphone exposes—but we are limited by it, too. I live in a city that is a land of ports, named after Portland, Maine, marking the travel of the English east to west, the shape of a particular way of knowing place.

One small thing I know is that English holds only one word for grizzly bear, fewer words than Ichishkiin provides, and the fact that grizzly bears no longer roam Oregon leads me to hope that Ichishkiin and other languages of this land might help me know this place. English fails to differentiate between the animals with heartbeats and the animals in legends, and our relations are circumscribed as such. English generalizes the parts of the salmon that Ichishkiin more precisely names. This land has its languages, some of which no living person nurtures forward. I suspect that I am closed off to some of the land's vibrancy as long as my words and syntax are in English, the language of these poetry investigations.

2.UPTICK

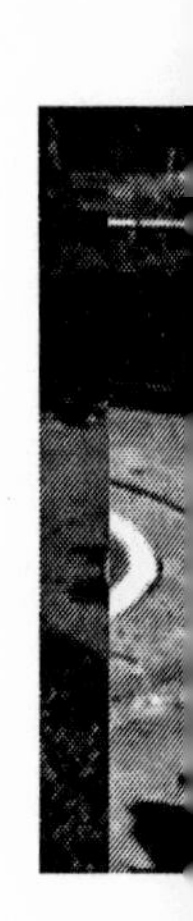

greetings from this hot future
broadcasting empire waste

the newscast carols loudly

pining for lushness, I observe greenery
green as winter

am I viewing the past or the future?

recognition bends

a centigrade uptick—
crops, deserted in desert dust
mountains melting, run-off rising
cities flooded, cars rusted low
large oceans larger
a flood of liquidity
houses inhospitable
& afloat

we try to eat & riot
in scarcity

we try to drink

sometimes with gusto

worrying conversations forward
shy raconteurs
standing in the backyard
distilling our liquor like neighbors
water strained through the grains

I don't expect he will be cruel
take care, though

bountiful bounty
sudden sun on a Sunday
suspect scarcity

there are so many of us
afoot—take care

some of us picking berries to bring to the table
some of us jetting berries from nation to nation
jetting nation to nation

Haitians are importing
rice & sugar, hungering
for what once grew nearby

some of us seeking return
on investments

the dispassionate rote
fury of financiers

up next: 'making a killing on the global food crisis'

the rulers, on the make
a frolic for the camera

profit, poverty

the dispassionate rote
fury of bankers banking
on our disengaged
engagements

in the use of the, in the many of the, in the use of the
in the many of the

that circle is showing the behavior of a sun

sun inked out
is night

in the land of the, in the land of the many
by the hand of the few

taking a risk
on the uptick

at all hours, someone is laboring
centigrade uptick
a rise in temp
work

in the land of the many
by the hand of the few

bailing
on the downturn

subprime
landgrab
meltdown

free speech ends when I call
fire in a crowded theater

but there is a fire

a burn is full of feeling
& it is in this time
I am alive
to love you

this is not puffer fish jetted from Japan

this is not Atlantic salmon, trucked from sea to sea

not cod, lobster, squid far flung

this is the jeweled among us, water breathers
small smelt
from nearby streams

nearness is knowledge
touching the fish touches back

a helping second

a New Year's second
spacious in the year's spate
of productive seconds

what is left open
is left open

the birds' carbon bodies fly in the carbon sky
& skywriting is taxable
in this time I am alive
with you

dry wind yields to rain
& some earth fills with wetness

more wetness is more river

more river forms to flood

here flood was damming:
the power to derive power

din of trucks in picnic weather

a mountain is a picture for us citydwellers
remembering to wave
a picture for us citydwellers in the sidesky

imagine, no reimagine, a municipal source of power

like flags, some of us leaning toward
some leaning away

one nation forced-floods over others
a dammed river over a waterfall

forced flooding, a dam slammed down
where thousands of years people
dipnetted salmon

presidential candidates flirt
with breeching dams

after the election Celilo Falls
will still be still

count us with the former ice
count us with the warming sea
count us with the strident storms

still—

count us in

acknowledgments

remember to wave poetry walk

This project was built, walked, conversed. Thank you to those who walked this poem many times: Jules Boykoff, Jessica Wahnetah, Neal Sand, Meg Eberle Ainsworth, Andrea Murray, Alicia Cohen, Pascale Cohen Fisher, Tom Fisher, David Abel, Sue Schoenbeck, Marjorie Pratt. Morning dew, fog, dusk, bats. Thank you Valerie Otani, for building the Torii, dogtags chiming where the walk begins.

And thank you to everyone who walked with me on September 28, 2008, the sun's heat intense as our walk ended; and everyone in Penelope Scambly Schott's walking group who joined me on January 10, 2009, bundled for frost. Thank you to Rodney Koeneke, Andrea Murray, David Abel, Jen Coleman, and Allison Cobb for performing bits of this walk-poem with me. Thank you to Jessica Wahnetah for dreaming up and building chimes with me, and ringing those chimes at chosen moments during the walk. Thank you to the impromptu ode poets, whose words I misheard and "translated": Colin Green, Larkin Smith, Sam Lohmann, James Yeary, Michaela Curtis-Joyce, Cat Tyc, Andrea Murray, David Abel, Penelope Scambly Schott, Zach Springer, Rodney Koeneke, Alicia Cohen, Bethany Ides, Joseph Bradshaw, Pam Hickman, Mark Hue, Sandi Nunn, Jesse Morse, Ethan Morse, Stacey Halpern, and Lisa Serrano. Thank you to Neal Sand for video documentation.

The Oregon Historical Society provided the *Evacuazette* featured in this poem-walk (and the Densho archive gave me access to most of the other *Evacuazettes* I read) as well as the "Resident Handbook Vanport," and the Oregon Nikkei Legacy Center provided the image of the "Instructions to all Persons of Japanese Ancestry." Thank you to Tiago DeJerk for creating the stencil of the Roller Derby skater, and to Draggin Lady for providing it. Thank you to Rocket Mean of the Rose City Rollers who arranged for me to attend a Roller Derby practice, and to all the Rollers who lent their autographs to this book. Thank you to Jules Boykoff who photographed the image at the site of the "Mud Slough Ode," as well as the final walking image in this book. I photographed all the other images, most at the walk's location, although the names "Clara Yokota" and "Betty Yamashiro" are carved in stone near Tule Lake, California, among petroglyphs and the Japanese and English added during the 1942-1946 internment years. I photographed the fisherman outside the Rose Garden Arena in northeast Portland.

The haiku was written by Shizuku Uyemaruko, a member of the Tule Lake Valley Ginsha, while she was interned at Tule Lake. It was reprinted from *May Sky: There Is Always Tomorrow* (Compiled and Translated by Violet Kazue de Cristoforo, Sun & Moon Press, 1997). Other source text comes from the PODS website sales materials and the Oregon Department of Human Resources DHS Environmental Toxicology Program website.

Thank you to the Regional Arts & Culture Council for a grant that supported this work.

So much depends on so much labor. Thank you Matt Love for engaged editing of the opening essay, and for publishing it in *Citadel of the Spirit* (Nestucca Spit Press 2009). Thank you Sam Lohmann for creating broadsides for the walk and publishing some of this walk in *Peaches & Bats*, and Jesse Morse for staging a reading of that work. Thank you to the Spare Room Collective for hosting the first walk, and Penelope Scambly Schott for hosting the second. Thank you to Samantha Giles at Small Press Traffic, Carla Perry and everyone at Writers on the Edge, and Zoë Skoulding and Ian Davidson at Bangor University, Wales, for staging readings, and the Nonsite and Belladonna Collectives and the Placing Poetry Colloquium for making possible discussion of this work. Thank you to Lacey Hunter for publishing some of the walk in *West Wind Review*, and David Wolach, Lionel Lintz, and Eden Schulz for publishing the map in *Wheelhouse*.

Thank you to Henry Sakamoto for discussing memories of the Portland Assembly Center; Bob Van Dyk for research on the Oregon Constitution; Gayle Moffitt, Charlotte Johnson, Steve Sand, and my dad, Joe Sand, for stories; and Beverly Dahlen, Jim Dine, Michael and Kathleen Glaser, and Diana Michener for conversations that matter to this writing. I walk with the engaged awareness of other walks and poetic investigations, too many to list here, but I do wish to call attention to David Buuck for his Bay Area Research Group in Enviro-aesthetics, and Lawson Inada for his documentary poem, "Legends from Camp," both of which inform this walk-poem, as do my ongoing conversations with Laura Elrick and Kristin Prevallet about poetry, performance, and public space, and as do my years of shared words with Jules Boykoff, who does so much to sustain space for me to work.

uptick

I wrote this poem as I viewed and reviewed a home-movie shot by William Cheney, a machine shop operator and inventor. The movie is a montage of scenes from the Pacific Northwest of the United States in the 1930s and 40s (William Cheney Motion Picture Collection, Oregon Historical Society, MI 01477). Thank you to Michele Kribs at the Oregon Historical Society for preparing the footage, and for permission to use the images.

I performed an early version of this poem as part of the NeoBenshi reading in Portland, Oregon, May 3, 2008. Thank you Konrad Steiner for tremendous labor and vision regarding the NeoBenshi movement, and to Rodney Koeneke for stewarding that movement in Portland. Thank you to Stephanie Young, who created a chapbook of this work for the Dusie Kollektiv 2008, and to Susana Gardner for her dusie vision. I handed out a broadside with a selection of "uptick" at the PACE action launched by CA Conrad and Frank Sherlock for the Econvergence in Portland, Oct. 3, 2009.

through attention to the
elsewhere & erstwhile
it is here & in this time
I am alive to love you

Kaia Sand is the author of a poetry collection, INTERVAL (Edge Books 2004), a Small Press Traffic Book of the Year, and co-author with Jules Boykoff of LANDSCAPES OF DISSENT: GUERRILLA POETRY and PUBLIC SPACE (Palm Press 2008), and she has created several chapbooks through the Dusie Kollektiv. Her poems LOTTO and TINY ARCTIC ICE comprise the text of two books in Jim Dine's HOT DREAMS series (Steidl Editions 2008). She lives in Portland, Oregon, with Jules Boykoff and their daughter, Jessica.